A LONG ROAD TO THE ALTAR

BY: R.D. SOLOMON JR.

A Long Road to the Altar

by Rowdy D. Solomon, Jr.

Dedication

This book is dedicated to all

believers and nonbelievers.

TABLE OF CONTENTS

CHAPTER ONE: BEFORE

CHRIST

As I stand here and

take a whiff of the cool night

air from my porch, I inhale

with my eyes closed,

remembering where I once

was and who I used to be.

Then, I exhale, opening my

eyes to see how far God has

brought me from. I look at

my wife then I look at my

kids and all I say is my

gosh.... Sometimes it feels

like they have been through

more than me from just

simply trying to bear with

me. Oh, please excuse me, let

me introduce myself. My

name is Shakir Davis. I am

33 years old and I am a

newly-found born again

Christian. My road to the

altar wasn't an easy one. For

a while I felt like I was going

in circles trying to get there.

Most thought I would never

walk down the aisle and give

my life back to Christ, but

here I am. If you don't mind,

I'd like to share my story with

you....

      You see, I have

always been a hardworking

man. I have always been

organized and responsible

and I have always taken care

of business. It would be safe

to say my success made me a

bit arrogant and ignorant. I

was working at a power plant

at the time located on the

outskirts of the city.

Cheyenne, Wyoming isn't

very popular, but it was very

peaceful and I would not

change my origin for the

world. I had the American

dream. However, I never

realized that being so

hardworking was also going

to be my downfall. My

beliefs were simply work

hard, live life, retire and reap

the benefits. My wife Camile

however…let's just say you

couldn't keep her out of the

church. Every time the doors

were open she was there. Not

only was she in the choir, but

she also was an usher on third

Sundays and she was the

assistant director of the dance

ministry. She took my kids

as well. My son Tristen, who

was 7 at the time, was a part

of the children's choir. My

daughter Shakira, who was 9

at the time, was as well, but

her passion was dancing.

Sadly, I had never seen them

use their gifts because I could

not gather up the intestinal

fortitude to go to church

myself. Then one day, that

question came up and my

wife finally wanted to talk.

Shakira was dancing

the next coming Sunday. She

had a solo part where she

would be dancing on her

own. That's when Camile

asked me, "When are you

going to come to church with

us? You promised me you

would come and the kids are

starting to wonder if they

have to go or not if you don't

go." I'll never forget that

moment. I felt the compelling guilt drop into my stomach like the gulp of beer I swallowed before I answered her question. I could only reply with, "Baby, I'm coming okay? Just tell the kids I work on Sundays right now. It's not that I don't want to go but…" "Don't worry about it. Just don't worry

about it." She replied

knowing I was trying to come

up with an excuse. She

walked away from me

shaking her head in

disappointment and dismay. I

look back now and I can't

believe I asked my own wife

to lie to my kids. I also

cannot believe I was trying to

lie to her, knowing she could

see straight through me.

Afterwards, I felt too guilty.

I remember Camile

and me talking in our

bedroom more about going to

church. She said, "Baby, God

is not happy with us. It was

cool when we were dating,

but we are married now. We

are unequally yoked. I want

all of my blessings from God.

I want you to have the same."

I don't remember much after

that. All I remember is I was

angry beyond measure. I

stood up, and I apparently

blacked out.

I woke up that

evening groggy and hung

over. I had 14 missed calls

from my job, all from my

boss himself. The kids were

play wrestling in the living

room. Camile was sitting on

the edge of the couch crying

and mumbling with her arms

folded rocking back and

forth. She had a black eye. I

exclaimed, "Camile, what happened!?! Who hit you!?!" She sat for a while and stared at the television. Her bottom lip started to tremble. Then turned and looked at me slowly and said, "You need to stop drinking." My heart nearly jumped out of my chest. I looked at my kids and instantly felt so low and so

bad. I wanted to end it all

right then. I told them to go

to their rooms while I tried

my best to apologize to

Camile. It was to no avail. So

from that day forward I

started sleeping on the couch

because she would lock the

room door at night. In my

heart I knew I needed help,

but like most, I thought I was

strong enough to kick my

drinking habit on my own,

the first of my many

mistakes.

CHAPTER TWO: RELAPSE

Summer months were

turning to fall months and

that's what it seemed like I

was doing. My drinking

problem was growing worse

by the day. It got so bad that I

was coming home every

night, going straight to the

refrigerator and grabbing a

beer. As time went on I

started to stash them in the

trunk of the car in a cooler

and next to the refrigerator

for quicker access. When I

came home at night, total

silence would fill the house.

My kids always ran into their

rooms when I would come from work. I would catch a glimpse of their faces and they would always be stricken with fear. I would often sit and feel a deep depression hit me because I knew I had a problem. There was a yearning for me to get this habit under control but things felt so good just the

way they were.

It was as if being

intoxicated was my norm, my

perfect world and my safe

haven. It came to a point

where I wasn't even

comfortable being sober

anymore. Then I made the

dumbest decision of my life. I

decided I would try to kick

my habit by trying out

another habit, hoping I would

stop drinking and then kick

that habit with no problem.

My co-worker, Jimmy had

me try some cocaine with

him one day during our

lunchbreak. The rush from it

made me feel like a

superhero, but only for a

short time. I did not want to

admit that I was relying on a

drug to deal with my

problems, so I did my best to

keep it a secret, even though I

felt myself lashing out even

more at my wife and now my

kids. It was definitely worse

than when I was drinking and

high on the cocaine at the same time. I was speeding up and slowing down. My heart was racing and I felt like I was moving slow. I needed help like no other, yet my pride would not let me admit it. Eventually, I stopped drinking because the cocaine gave me a better feeling.

When my wife noticed I

wasn't buying beer anymore,

I didn't have the heart to tell

her I was doing drugs, so I

told her work was stressing

me and I didn't want to drink

to handle it. The urge started

to get the best of me.

Awakening in cold sweats

and not eating seemed like a

holy ritual. Yet, my wife stayed by my side. I knew she knew, but we never spoke of it to one another.

Camile became the breadwinner. However, working at a clothing at a clothing store as a retail associate didn't pay everything. I felt so bad. I couldn't function at work anymore. Even being under the influence wasn't helping anymore. My hands would shake uncontrollably and I would often feel like I was going to have a heart attack. My boss started to notice my performance was slipping and decided to start giving me less hours to have some

time to myself. However, I

used that time to enjoy the

very thing that was

destroying me all the more. I

would use back alleys and

park the car there and just

smoke to my heart's content.

Of course, I couldn't tell my

wife about my boss cutting

my hours, so I told her they

made budget cuts and a

couple of other employees

and I had to use some

vacation days to compensate.

The look on her face could

pierce diamonds because

once again I knew she could

see right through my lies.

      I felt like I was losing

my mind, and I knew I was

losing my family. Shakira

was afraid of me now and

Tristen would often lash out

at school because of all the

drama I brought to the house.

Camile couldn't bear it any

longer, nor did I wish for her

or my kids to. Regardless of

my habit, I dearly loved my

family. The kids went to live

with their maternal

grandmother, and my wife

eventually left me to do the

same. I knew it was best even

though it hurt me to my heart.

I remember sitting on the bed

crying and almost vomiting

from being sick and tired of

the life that made me feel so

good and bad but...I was just

getting started with my

endeavors.

CHAPTER THREE:

SINKING FAST

I wish I could erase the day my boss pulled me into the office along with Jimmy. I could feel my heart pulsating through the temples of my skull as we entered and sat down in front of his prized long Oakwood desk.

All I could think was, "Please let this be a promotion or some type of warning for the both of us". He began to ask us questions pertaining to how our home lives were and how our families were. Then he asked if we had savings plans, accounts and money saved up for a rainy day. My first thought was the plant

was getting ready to move or

something and either we

could drive further to work or

transfer because there were

many locations of this

company in the city. It didn't

cross my mind that both of us

would be receiving pink slips

for our performances over the

past six months. He told us

we that lost the plant

thousands of dollars

collectively and budget cuts

had already been made. Our

positions were the first two.

There was nothing he could

do to save our jobs or our

reputations. We had truly let

the plant and our

subordinates down, not to

mention our families. What

was I going to tell Camile?

Jimmy tried to save my job

by saying, "Sir, the reason

Shakir has been to out of it

lately is because I have not

been doing my job. He has

been helping me to try to get

it together. Please, don't fire

him." He knew how much I had to lose. My boss replied "I understand. Though this is a hard task for me to carry out, it is not my decision on either one of you. It is the company's. Again I am truly sorry and sympathetic for this misfortune. I wish you both the best in the future."

Now I couldn't even

support the bad habit that had

been making me feel so good.

I went home and destroyed

the house to symbolize how I

felt inside. I was truly a

wreck, a tornado. Emotional

and confused was I. I didn't

know what to do so I sat

outside on the porch and

thought about my next move.

I needed money to get a fix. I

felt so broken internally. I

called Jimmy but I didn't get

an answer. I called some of

my ex co-workers to see if

they had heard from him.

That's when I found out that

Jimmy was killed later that

same night. I guess he had

messed around with the

wrong people, so I couldn't

go to him for anything. I

went for a long walk around

the neighborhood and ended

up in the park. My head was

throbbing. I began to feel sick

al of a sudden. All I wanted

was to turn back the hands of

time. Camile wasn't returning

any of my calls. This was a

time I was just begging,

yearning, to hear her voice,

so I kept calling just to hear it

on the answering machine. I

missed the life I had. I missed

my kids, home cooked meals

and even my arguments I

would have with Camile.

Nevertheless, my high

was apparently more important at the time. Yes, even more important than my house and my family. Time had gone by so fast that I failed to remember that I didn't have a job. Needless to say I couldn't pay rent. I sold most of the things I had in the house for cheap for fixes.

They were reasonable prices

to say the least. So, now I

was out on my feet and out

on the street.

I walked the streets,

thinking of people I could

call on. My parents were

deceased. The rest of my

family was not an option

because we never got along

and Camile's mom didn't

take to me to well. I recalled

a nearby homeless shelter I

took my cousin to until she

was able to get housing.

Sadly, to say, she was still

there. She vouched for me,

but there was one rule...I had

to be clean. Upon getting my

room, the first thing I did was

put my family's picture on the

wall. That was my

motivation.

Within two weeks, I

had a job interview at a steel

making company that was

within walking distance from

the shelter. I just knew I was

about to turn my life around.

I just knew this was my

chance. However, jittered and not able to sit still, I threw up twice, heaved and couldn't make it to the interview. I was so bummed and so careless that I lit up as I was walking back to the shelter. Not even a block from the shelter, I was arrested for possession of cocaine and being under the influence.

They took me to the shelter to

see if I was really staying

there like I had said. They

found my stash under my

mattress at the shelter and

tested me when they cuffed

me and took me in. Still, I

thought hard work and

dedication would get me back

to where I needed to be. I had

nothing to do with two years

possibly in front of me as a

sentence I had to serve, so I

began to think of ways that

would potentially help

shorten my sentence such as

being a model prisoner or

becoming involved in

different programs. However,

I knew the first thing was

getting clean.

CHAPTER FOUR: BEHIND BARS

Knowing that my

actions and bad decisions tore

my family apart saddened

me. What hurt even more was

seeing the pain in my

children's eyes and hearing

their questions to which I had

no easy answers to cut like a
knife. Camile told me they
were asking questions like,
"Why doesn't Daddy live
with us anymore?' and,
'What did Daddy do wrong?'
'Does Daddy still love us?
When is Daddy coming
home?' Each question cut me
deeper and deeper to the soul.

What hurt the most is when

they came to see me. My

daughter said she overheard

Camile on the phone saying

she enjoyed her date the other

night and she couldn't wait

for them to go out again. I

tried my best to assure them

that everything would be

okay, that they did nothing

wrong, that I still loved them

and their mother and that I

made some bad decisions that

called for some rough

consequences. I knew then

that I had to get myself

together. I had to get out of

my own way. The problem

was however, I dug a hole so

deep for myself that I

couldn't get out…or so I thought.

After their visit, I had more time to do what I had been doing the last few months…think. After crying, sobbing and burning for the life I once knew, I decided enough was enough and I needed to get some help. You see, my father wasn't always

around when I was growing

up. I didn't want my children

to say the same about me. I

finally had the heart and

mind to get myself together

for my family. After what my

daughter said, I didn't know

if my wife would ever

forgive me let alone give me

another chance, but I
definitely was not going to
give up on us. I was
determined to try with
everything in me to prove I
am the man she once loved
and wanted to spend the rest
of her life with.

The next morning
after breakfast, I asked the

warden were there any

programs to help me with my

drug and alcohol problem. He

told me go to the library and

sign up for the next meeting

for Drugs Anonymous. There

I met some really nice

people. We shared our stories

of how we got to the place

we were in and what made us

decide it was time to get

some help. Two guys

specifically really touched

me. They had overcome their

addictions, but still attended

the meetings to make sure

they stayed on the right track

and also to try to make a

difference in the lives of

others by sharing their

stories. They started talking about how God used tragic situations to change their lives around.

The first man lost his family in a car accident. He was driving his family home from a dinner one night and he was drunk. He knew he had consumed too many drinks, but he decided to

drive home anyway against

his wife's wishes. He ran the

traffic light and his vehicle

was hit on the passenger's

side. His son was killed

instantly and his wife

eventually died in the

hospital a couple of days later

due to head trauma. Needless

to say that's how he ended up

in jail. After losing

everything he had, one would

think that would have made

him go into a deeper

depression, but instead this

unfortunate and unexpected

event drew him closer to

God.

The other man's

incident wasn't as tragic

because it didn't involve him

directly, but he did witness a

family losing their house in a

fire. He was riding down the

street in his car, high as the

dickens from a freshly

smoked blunt when he saw

smoke and as he kept driving,

he saw the flames and the

house that was on fire. He

saw a woman and some

children he assumed to be

hers standing in the driveway

crying. He pulled over, called

911 and got out of his

vehicle. He told the woman

that firemen were on the way

and that he would stay until

they left to make sure

everything was okay. In

distraught, she thanked him

and stated that she and her

children had just gotten home

from visiting a relative and

saw that the house was on

fire. He replied that he was

glad no one was home when

it happened and that everyone

was safe. To that, she replied

that she couldn't get in touch

with her husband. When she

left the house, he was home

and he could possibly still be

inside. When the firemen got

to the house some

immediately started to put out

the fire and some went inside

to see if anyone else was

inside. Unfortunately, the

woman's husband was

inside…dead. It was later

determined that her husband

was high at the time of the

fire; too high to notice that

the house was even on fire. It

was also determined by

police that the man that was

sharing his story smelled like

marijuana, and the rest is

history. He was arrested for

possession and intoxication.

He was also half drunk. That

was his wake up call. Getting

high wasn't worth losing his

life or even the lives of his

family. It was that incident

that changed his life forever.

He became saved later on.

His family joined a Bible

based church and they've

been serving God ever since,

waiting on the day for him to

come home.

After hearing their

stories, I began to wonder if

there was anything to this

God that these men and my

wife had been talking about.

Meeting these men was the

beginning of a new life for me. I knew nothing would change overnight, but I was definitely prepared for the journey to a better life. One that included my children…and my wife.

CHAPTER FIVE:

THE TEST

After the meeting, I
went back to my cell. My
cellmate, Tyrone, was sitting
on his bunk humming. He
had always hummed and he
never said much, but this
particular day I noticed him

reading as he hummed. I looked at the front of the book and lo and behold, it was a Holy Bible. So, after mustering up enough courage, I asked him, "Hey man, do you believe in God?" He replied, "With all of my heart brother," without even looking up at me. This struck an interesting conversation

between us because I never

knew Tyrone believed in God

up until then. I had never

seen him with his Bible out,

but then again, I did go to bed

early most nights. So I asked,

"So how did you end up in

here then?" He replied again

and said, "Ain't nobody

perfect man. You see I found Jesus when I was thrown in here. Even though I am in here for life, I know Christ has covered my sins with his blood." After seeing the look of astonishment on my face, he continued and said, "I guess I have to tell you my story. You see, knowing I was sentenced to life I figured,

why not take my life and get

it over with? So I sharpened

the end of a toothbrush on the

bed rail until it was pointed

and tried to kill myself. I was

unsuccessful obviously. I

missed all of my vital organs

and heart. That's when I

found Jesus." Upon telling

me this, he showed me the

scar on his chest to prove his

story to me. "My old cellmate

was Christian. He prayed

with me and showed me the

way."

I felt something drop

into the pit of my stomach. It

was as if God was trying to

tell me something but I was

not sure what it was nor if it was really God or not. So, I asked him, "Do you attend church at the chapel in here? Before he could answer, I asked more questions out of the assumption due to his facial expression. "Would you mind studying with me and showing me the way?"

Tyrone started crying

instantly, as if it were second

nature. I asked him, "Why

are you crying? Did I offend

you? I'm sorry." He said,

"No need to apologize

brother. You see I have been

praying for God to use me

and now…here you are. Look

at God! This brought tears to

my eyes as well, even though

I still did not understand

completely. Then, Tyrone

gave me a hug and I had my

first ever Bible study right

there in the jail cell, which is

why I hold Jeremiah 29:11

near and dear to me.

Even though I was

learning the ways of the

Bible and attending my

meetings regularly, it did not

make trying to rehabilitate

and do right any easier. It

actually made it a little harder

to deal with. Drugs and

drama were all around me.

Seeing these things often

forced me to flash back to

days of old when I was on

drugs. The feeling, the rush,

and the escape overcame me

to a point where I lost it

during lunch one day. I had a

nervous breakdown.

Tyrone was by my

bedside when I woke up. He

asked me, "What happened

man? What's wrong?" The

only response I had for him

was another question, "Why is it we are trying to do right but all of these who aren't are reaping the benefits? They get special privileges, shoes, clothes, cigarettes, and even people doing stuff for them like their maids. What do we have? Where is our reward for doing right?" Tyrone smiled and lowered his head.

He said, "You sound like

King Asaph before he went

into the sanctuary." I was

lost. I had no idea what he

was talking about. It made

me mad when he did that

because I wasn't as inclined

on the Bible as he was. "Read

Psalms 73 and get better

brother." Then, he left

humming, which I still never

understood why he was

humming or what he was

humming.

CHAPTER SIX: THE RELEASE

I can't say I felt my best coming out of that hospital bed and back into my cell. Walking out of that place was like walking out of freedom and into Hell again. I felt myself crying internally because I felt so free for that

time period. Yet, being

handcuffed to a bed rail isn't

exactly free, is it? Tyrone

gave me a hug as I entered

the cell. "Welcome home

brother," he said. Of course,

it didn't feel like much of a

welcome regardless of what

he did. "Did you read the

verses I gave you?" he asked

me. I couldn't lie.

"Look man, I know

that you mean well, but I just

don't see where all of this

God business is really taking

me. I mean, c'mon, I can't

see him, I can't hear him, and

I can't even call him. So why

should I believe He's going

to take care of me?" Tyrone once again looked at me in disappointment. "This is why I told you to read the verses. What did you do while you were in the hospital? No, wait…let me guess. You sulked in your own depression by thinking about your family and all that has happened, right? You made it up in your mind that this is it and there is no way to change that. You're thinking you might as well join those who have luxuries in here and live the 'good life', right?"

I was stuck. Everything he said he was right about. However, me being a man I said, "No, I was actually thinking about getting out of here, seeing my wife and kids and doing the right thing. Shows how much you know!" He replied, "So how do you plan on doing that brother? Do you plan on doing that with your own plan or God's plan?" Again I was stuck. "I don't know

man. I don't know. I'm

just…" Tyrone interrupted,

"You're right where I used to

be. I gave up when I should

have kept going. I lost

everything and ended up

here. Then I found God right

before I was going to take my

own life. Just like I had

someone there for me, I am

going to be there for you,

whether you like it or not!"

Tears uncontrollably

fell from my face as I moved

to the bed and sat back on it.

For the first time since I had

been in jail, I actually felt…I

felt pain. I felt guilt. I felt a

deep mourning within me

like no other. However, it

seemed as if the more I cried,

the lighter my burdens

became. Before I knew it, I

called on God for the first

time. "God, I need you. I

don't know if you can hear

me or not. My wife knows

you. My kids know you. I

know I have never called on

you before, but if they know

you, then you must be alright.

I've been through the fire and

right now I am standing in

the rain. I want my life back.

Please God, if you hear me. I

just want my life back. I'm

not asking for money, fame

or even for every day to be

great. I just want my life

back. God I'm begging

you!"

Tyrone cried along

with me. Imagine two grown

men crying and hugging. It

sounds kind of gay, doesn't

it? To add to the mix, Tyrone

actually started singing. He

finally put words to that

seemingly annoying

humming he always used to do. He sang, "What a friend we have in Jesus, all our sins and griefs to bear. What a privilege to carry everything to God in prayer." Then the warden told him to shut up. We laughed. "It's going to be okay brother," Tyrone reassured "Just hold on.

God's got you. Are you ready to read the verses now?" After a head-nod of yes, we got out our Bibles and began to study.

CHAPTER SEVEN: THE

SCHOLAR

The Bible seemed a

lot like poetry to me. It was

almost as if it was one big

encyclopedia of metaphors

that confused me at first. To

help me understand, Tyrone

would often quote a phrase

from the present age we are

living in so I would get how

it fit into my life. I began to

listen so much to where I

began relate it to my life for

myself. I can say I truly

became a student of the

Bible. It got to a point where

I was starting to memorize

verses and their meaning and

even figure out there was

more than one meaning at

times depending on at what

point you were reading it in

your life and from what

viewpoint you take it. I was

more than proud of myself

and probably even a little full

of myself. Tyrone was proud

of me as well, until one

unexpected incident

occurred…

I was eating lunch

with Tyrone when a gang

member came to the table

and slapped my Bible from

the table. My heart

immediately started racing

and anger built within. "Get

up sissy! Fight!" he said. So I

got up but Tyrone told me,

"Just pick the Bible up and sit

down. He's not worth it."

"Shut up! This is between me

and him!" he yelled at

Tyrone. That's when I

couldn't bare the disrespect

any longer. I lost it. I threw

the rest of my food in his face

and flew across the table.

Then, I used my lunch tray to

try to cave his skull in. I saw

his fellow gang members

from across the mess all

staring me down as I was

handcuffed and taken to the

hole. I knew I had it coming

after what I had done to him.

I was ready.

I didn't realize how

much power and pull Tyrone

had around there. He stopped

the warden and asked to have

a word with me. He also

raised his hand as he looked

at the gang members and they

nodded and walked away.

"What was that all about!?!

You know the only reason

you are going to be okay is

because they owe me a favor,

right!?! Look, it's one thing

to read the word. It's another

thing to live it! I can't

believe…look, I'll see you in

a month brother." Tyrone

said. I still have no idea how

he knew I was going to be

thrown in the hole for a

month. It was usually three to

six months for fighting.

Lucky for me, I was

able to keep my Bible, so I

had something to keep me

busy while I was in there.

The only thing that was

bothering me was I didn't

have Tyrone to keep me

company and to teach me

words and such I didn't

know, or to confirm that my

meaning of a verse was the

right meaning. It was a long

month indeed for me. Every

day, all I could think about

was the way I acted and how

I let Tyrone and myself not to

mentions my family down. I

was so disappointed in

myself. I didn't know what to

do. I felt so bad. I felt like I

had let God down most of all.

There I was, feeling

again…lower than last time.

So I did the only thing I knew

to do. I studied. I searched

and searched for an answer

on how to be forgiven by

God. I wasn't sure if I was

saying the word correctly, but

I found where the Bible said

to repent and I will be

forgiven. I couldn't wait for

that month to be over so I

could ask Tyrone what that

meant.

CHAPTER EIGHT:

FORGIVENESS

Tyrone was reading as I was entering the cell from the hole. For the first time in my life, I was happy to see bars instead of a door. He simply said, "Welcome back brother. He sat back on the bunk, put his back to the wall, and asked, "How do you feel?" In a low temperate tone, I fell to my knees and busted out in tears from keeping that low feeling bottled up inside. "Man, I feel so bad Tyrone. All month what I did to that guy has been on my mind. I want to go apologize, but I know that

is out of the question. What

should I do man!?! I searched

the Bible on what to do for

God to forgive me, but I

don't understand. It said

something about repatance."

Of course, I was saying the

word wrong and Tyrone

corrected me after laughing at

me for about five minutes

straight, "It's repentance

/rəˈpentəns/ brother. I will tell

you all about it. If you are

sincere in seeking

forgiveness, simply ask God

for it in prayer. Then, you

must do your best to never do

that thing again."

Obviously, I did like

most do. So, I asked, "So all we have to do it ask God for forgiveness and he grants it just like that? So basically I can do what I want to do and just ask forgiveness anytime, right?" Tyrone chuckled even more and replied, "No brother. Once again, you have to be sincere, meaning you have to mean it. It has to

come from the heart" I was

then starting to understand

more of what Tyrone meant

by living the life of a

Christian, or at least I thought

I did. At that point I at least

had the concept down

packed. It was hard, but I did

feel better. Look at

me…again with the feeling.

So I got down on my

knees, but before I began to

pray Tyrone stopped me and

asked, "Why did you get on

your knees?" I told him,

"This is what my wife and

kids used to do every night. I

figured this is how you

prayed. Am I doing

something wrong?" Tyrone said, "You can pray on your knees, but it's not a necessity. However, to show how humble you are in your repentance, stay there for now." "What do I say?" I asked Tyrone. "Say what's on your heart." He told me. So then I prayed, "Our Father, which art in Heaven,

Hallowed by thy name. God,

I come before you asking for

forgiveness for my actions. I

let my anger get the best of

me. I hurt a man. I ask now

for forgiveness and I pray I

can move on from this. In

Jesus' name, amen."

I didn't feel relieved

right away, but as time went

on throughout the day I

started to feel better. I saw

the man again that day and

apologized to him. He didn't

respond to me. He just

looked, nodded and went on

about his way. I am not sure

what that meant, but I did

feel better after doing so. I

was definitely growing, but I

had a lot of growing to do.

However, I was not ready for

what happened next.

CHAPTER NINE: DO

UNTO OTHERS

I tossed and turned all night long. I kept waking up because of the nightmare of ultimately losing my family for good. I kept dreaming the same dream over and over. We would be having a family picnic and then all of a

sudden a huge storm would

come, wipe them out, and

leave me standing there. I

wasn't sure what to do or

how to interpret that. I was

trying to keep my breaths and

sighs down because I knew

Tyrone was sleeping. Yet, I

ended up waking him up

because I couldn't hold in the

tears and the wailing any

longer.

"What's wrong

brother? Are you okay?"

Tyrone said in concern as he

yawned in his groggy state. "I

don't know man, this

dream…." Before I could

continue, Tyrone interrupted

me and said, "If you really

want your family back, it's

not going to be easy. You will

have to go through quite a

bit, but I have faith in you as

you build your faith in Jesus.

Talk to God about it brother;

He will listen. Give the

situation to him and I

promise you will sleep better

than a soldier that has just

come home when you put it

in his hands." So, I did as

Tyrone told me, and it

worked like a charm, even

though I had a surprise

waiting on me the next

morning.

It was Thursday

again. Every Thursday is

visiting day. My wife didn't

show up with the kids this

time. I was hurt, but all I

could do was call later on

when I was allowed to. I at

least wanted to hear from

them if I didn't see them. As

I left the sitting area where so

many were crying,

conversing and smiling, I saw

the man I beat up with my

lunch tray. He was talking to

his significant other I had to

assume. He looked really

distraught. He looked like he

was begging and pleading

from his hand gestures and

the tears. The female seemed

to be unbothered by his

distraught state. She got up

and walked away. He was left

there, crying and weeping

drowning the table with his

tears.

I felt a tugging and

yearning in my spirit to do

something to at least try to

help, so I went over to him

and began to try to comfort

him, "Brother, I don't know

what you are going through, but all I am going to tell you is trust God. I know it sounds crazy but it is what I am doing now and I must say it's working for me. He is the way to getting my family back and he is also the way to fix your situation. Can I pray with you?" The man lifted his head, looked at me, got up,

and hit me in the face. I guess

I deserved that after what I

had done to him. When we

got back to the cell, Tyrone

asked me, "What happened to

your eye?" All I could say

was, "You know that verse

that says 'Do unto others as

you would have them do unto

you?'" Tyrone replied,

"Yeah, but what does that

have to do with your eye?" I

told him, "Something was

done unto me that I did unto

someone." When he put two

and two together Tyrone

laughed and said, "In a literal

sense that is hilarious, but I

see we still have a lot of

studying to do."

CHAPTER TEN: SET

BACK

It had been a year

now since I had been sitting

aimlessly in that forsaken

place called jail. It seemed

like the walls were closing in

more and more every day.

Yet, I was hopeful still

because of my knowledge of

God's word that I had now

attained. It was time. I was up

for my parole hearing. All I

had to do was continue to

keep my nose clean and keep

my mouth shut. I was more

than ready to see my family I

was ready to go home and

begin life anew. My court

date was the next day, so I talked to Tyrone about what I needed to do in regards to the hearing and how to conduct myself.

"Brother, all you need to do is sit there and look as sincere as you can. You have a really good chance on getting out of here early and starting your life over again

with your family. I am so

proud of you. You have truly

come a long way and I am

not just saying that." I was

encouraged and a bit

emotional by Tyrone's advice

and encouragement. "Thank

you for all you have done for

me brother. I would not have

made it to this point in my
life without you. Truth be
told, I probably would have
taken my own life or would
have gotten killed in here had
it not been for you." Tyrone
immediately corrected me,
"Brother thank God! He is
the reason any of us have
made it this far. Remember

what I told you and

everything will be just fine. I

expect a good report

tomorrow."

I felt kind of weird

because I didn't meet my

lawyer until I walked into the

room and sat down next to

him. We didn't even speak.

The case just started. So, I

was a bit skeptical on how he

was going to get me out of

jail if he had never met me

before. However, he did

sound eloquent and educated,

"Your honor, if I may, Mr.

Davis has been nothing shy

of a model citizen within

these prison walls. Though he

has had one incident some

months ago with a fellow

inmate, he has completely

turned his life around and is

even attending church here

which he plans to continue to

do with his family upon

release." However, the judge

seemed to be against me, "I

am aware of Mr. Davis'

complete 180, but his

incident cannot go unnoticed.

He sent that fellow inmate to

our hospital with a broken

nose and a fractured jaw.

Actions like this cannot and

will not be tolerated. We have

no choice but to deny parole

for now due to these horrific

actions. Case dismissed"

My hearing was quick

and simple. I felt my

heartbeat in my head as

everything around me went

silent. My muscles tightened

as I overflowed my face with

tears and emotion much like

the man that day when he lost

his love in the visitor's center

and hit me in the face. I was a

complete wreck. All hope

had gone flying out of the window for me when the gavel hit the desk. I got back to the cell and just laid there in silence. I had lost all direction.

Tyrone tried to cheer me up with more words of encouragement, "Cheer up man. Not too many people get it on the first try. You will

get it next time." I replied, "I

don't think I will get another

chance man. My lawyer said

it would be best to just do

this last year and get it over

with. I don't think I have the

patience nor the strength to

last another year away from

my family though. I don't

know what to do man."

"Tyrone replied, "Pray

brother and keep doing what

you're doing. It has not gone

unnoticed. With God…" I

interrupted and finally

snapped, "With God I'm

wasting my time! What has

all of this gotten me huh!?!

It's gotten me nothing but

another year here!" I caught

myself and thought about my

family and thought about

what I was saying. If my

family believed, I had to

believe. It was my only

chance and window to them.

"I'm sorry Tyrone. I just need

some sleep. I'll talk to you in

the morning." Tyrone prayed

for me out loud as I fell

asleep. For some reason his

voice soothed my soul that

night.

CHAPTER ELEVEN:

MIXED EMOTIONS

Awakening that next

day was like starting a new

file on a video game. I felt

like I was starting over my

sentence from the beginning,

even though I was halfway

through it. I had so many

questions for God, "God,

what do I do now? Which

way do I go? How much

longer do I have to be in

here? How is my family?" I

wanted to hold my wife. I

wanted to kiss my kids. I

wanted my family back. I felt

powerless because all I could

do was pray and stay on the

right track.

The next visiting day was very intense for me. I had an unexpected visitor along Camile and the kids this time. My mother-in-law decided she would tag along. Of course, I expected the worst seeing her. I was sure Camile was going to ask for a

divorce and full custody of
the kids. "Hey baby, how are
y'all?" Camile rolled her eyes
and said, "I think we should
be asking how you are."
"Daddy, how much longer
are you going to be on
vacation?" Shakira asked me
in anticipation. With a sigh
and holding back tears I said,

"Well sweetheart, it's up to my bosses when I can come home." I then turned to Tristen, placed my hand on his shoulder and said, "It won't be long son." He snatched and turned away from me with haste and buried his head in my mother-in-law's chest. She then said, "He will be okay

after a while. Just give him

some time." I said, "Mom, I

wasn't expecting to ever see

you on a visiting day." She

sighed and said, "If my

daughter is sticking by you

through all of this, then there

must be something about you

that's good. So, you also have

my support."

These words from my mother-in-law brought tears to my eyes once again. For the first time ever, I cried in front of my wife and kids. I couldn't hold my peace any longer. "God, I just want to thank you for bringing my family to me today, and allowing this barrier to be

broken between my

mother-in-law and me. Lord,

if you get me out of here, I

promise to do right and love

my family. Please God! I'm

tired! Get me out of here!"

I was making too much noise,

so the warden cut our visit

short. Before they left, my

mother-in- law told me,

"Keep trusting son. God will

see you through this whole

endeavor. Everything

happens on his time." As she

hugged me and gave me a

kiss on the cheek. Camile

said, "Keep your hand in

God's hands and keep your

nose clean. Don't give up

okay? We are with you and

we love you" The kids had

fallen asleep, so I kissed their

foreheads and was escorted

back to my cell. I didn't

know how to feel going back

to my cell. Was my

mother-in-law really for me,

or was she just supporting her

daughter like she had literally

stated? Why was my

daughter feeling one way and

my son, another? All I was

sure of is I was ready to go

home. That cell seemed to get

smaller by the day and as

much as I enjoyed having

Tyrone as a cellmate, I was

tired of talking to him while I

was using the bathroom in

the open.

CHAPTER TWELVE:

ROUND TWO

It had been six

months since I had been to

my last parole hearing. I had

a year left on my sentence

because of the incident now,

but now I was very hopeful. I

was so hopeful and confident

on getting out that I shaved,

pressed my uniform and tried

my best to look like a model

prisoner, a term I used lightly.

Yet, I was still nervous.

Anxiety was in every inhale

and exhale as I waited in the

holding cell pending my

hearing. Yet, I prayed from

my heart mentally until it was

time for me to go in.

My counsel came in with an officer. It was just the officer last time and he brought me into the hearing room. I knew then it was time. I quickly said in my mind, "God it's in your hands." I rose from my seat, straightened my uniform as much as I could while

handcuffed and proceeded to

the courtroom. All I could

think about was my family, a

chance at life once again and

finally leaving that cell never

to return. Yes, I would miss

Tyrone, but I knew I could

write and visit him. My

heartbeat was pulsating in my

head as my counsel talked to the headman. I saw many faces that didn't look good. I started to doubt a little, but I said a small prayer in my head while they continued on my conduct and behavior as they deliberated.

Then, all of a sudden I saw a smile from my counsel.

That was my light at the end

of the tunnel. I looked back

and saw Camile crying, my

kids jumping for joy and

even Tyrone who was

allowed to sit in was praising

God. Praying so hard and

being in my own world I

didn't realize that I had been

approved for parole. Tears

ran down my face

uncontrollably like a released

river of joy. I was trying to

muster up the voice and

eloquence to say thank you

Lord, but I couldn't through

the emotion. All I could do

was cry, sob, gather myself

and look to the future. It was

time to put my studies to the

test. Was I ready? Only time would tell.

As I was packing, Tyrone wanted to give me some nuggets to take home with me. "Brother this is another chance. I say that because God is a God of not just a second chance, but another chance. Use this to your advantage to not only

gain the trust and

encouragement of your wife,

but the trust and

encouragement of your

family. I pray you the richest

blessings out there. The

world has probably changed a

tad bit since you've been in

here, so don't be afraid.

Embrace it." With tears

rolling down his face he said,

"I never want to see you in

here again. Keep the faith

my brother. One more thing,

send a brother some beef

jerky if you can, will you? I

miss that!" We could do

nothing but laugh. "Brother, I

will send you all of the jerky

you want. Just keep the faith as well. I love you brother."

That was the first time in my life that I had ever said I loved another man. To my surprise, I did not feel gay or uncomfortable.

On another note, I did not know what to do or how to feel about going home.

Butterflies rumbled in my

stomach and so many

questions ran through my

head. I was so anticipated,

yet so scared. I did not know

what to expect, nor did my

family. This was going to be

a new experience indeed.

CHAPTER THIRTEEN: ADAPTATION PROBLEM

Walking out of those gates was like being released from the womb at birth. I was unaware of my surroundings but ready to go anywhere besides back in there. The sun nearly blinded me. I was free to do and say what I pleased. My mother-in-law was waiting for me at the end of the sidewalk to take me home. Shakira ran and hugged me. "Baby Girl! Oh, I have missed you so much! Where is your brother?" I asked. "He's back home with mom. He didn't want to come." That was a sign to me

I had some work to do, not

only with adapting to civilian

life again and trying to make

things right with my family,

but with also trying to gain

the trust of my wife and son

again.

"Let's go boy! You've

been inside those walls for

almost two years now. Now

they've let you out and you

act like you don't want to go.

There's no sense in looking at

them now. Let's go now!"

My mother-in-law said. I

picked my Shakira up and ran

to the car with excitement

filling my stomach and

anxiety filling my mind. I had

so many questions. What

does home look like? How

will Camile react to me? Will

I ever have a right

relationship with my son?

What does my mother-in-law

think of me? All of my

questions would be answered

in due time, but I wasn't

ready for some of the

answers I would receive.

The ride home was

the most beautiful experience

I had ever had. The scenery

was like taking a road trip to

a new location I had never

seen before. I enjoyed every

detail. I saw kids playing,

supermarkets, beautiful

women and even the smell of

the air was different. Shakira

was hopping around in the

backseat like an adolescent.

Her birthday was coming up

and she just kept naming off

things she wanted. To most it

would be annoying but since

it had been almost 2 years for

me since having an actual

conversation with my

daughter outside of jail walls,

I was enjoying every moment

of the usually annoying

antics. "Daddy I want an

iPhone 7, a laptop, the new

pink and white Jordan's…"

"Girl hush! Your mother

doesn't have money for all of

that!" I felt a low point drop

into my spirit as my

mother-in-law made that statement. "I'll do what I can Baby Girl" is all I could say.

"Now don't make a promise you can't keep. You're notorious for that." My mother-in-law said as she cut her eyes at me through the rearview mirror. I felt my anger building within me but

I remembered I was in her

car. She was the type to pull

over and make you walk, so I

kept my mouth shut. When

we pulled into the driveway

and turned off the car, my

heart nearly jumped out of

my chest. At first sight, I

thought my mother-in-law

had moved until she said,

"Now you're home. I expect

you to treat it as such. Don't

hurt my daughter again. Do

you hear me?" "Yes ma'am"

I said in a low tone. She gave

me quick hug and kicked

Shakira and me out of the car.

That was in indication to me

she was truly dealing with me

for Camile. Nevertheless, I

was home and it was time to

work.

As we walked to the

door and my mother-in- law

pulled off, Shakira knocked

because I was afraid to.

Seeing Camile's face as she

opened the door was like our

first date all over again. All

we could do was look and

stare at each other for a while

as Shakira ran into the house

past Camile yelling,

"Daddy's home! Daddy's

home!"

CHAPTER FOURTEEN:

THE EXPLOSION

When Camile opened

the door all of the way, I

slowly stepped in to what I

could now call home. I

immediately fell to my knees

and busted out in tears.

Camile placed her hands on

my shoulders and said, "It's going to be okay. Then she kissed me on my forehead and said, "C'mon, get up." Standing to my feet was hard. It felt like I had been to war and they just put me on the plane and shipped me home after a firefight. I was weak but I was at peace.

Shakira was so

excited to have me home that

she jumped on me as soon as

I was in the house well.

"Daddy, let me show you my

room! I have my own room

now!" I'm trying to dodge

furniture as she tries to pull

my arm out of the socket to

get to her room. "Alright,

alright slow down!" I pleaded

to her with chuckles within

my words. The room was

beautiful. The walls were

painted lavender and the

baseboards were blue. She

had her own closet, bed and

television. I had obviously

missed a lot in two years. It

took a bit for to take it all in.

Camile walked in

shortly after I took a glance

around the room. "This is

what hard work gets you,

right?" She said. "Yeah, I

suppose so." I said. Camile

blew up instantly. "You

haven't grown a bit since

you've been in there have

you!?! This is what God gets

you when you're faithful and
you serve him in good times
and bad!" After telling me
off, Camile went and sat on
the couch. I told Shakira to
stay in the room while I talk
to Camile. I went into the
living room to sit next to her
on the couch. "Where is
Tristen?" I asked her. "He's

at my mom's. He didn't want to be here when you got here."

I couldn't understand why Camile was so mad. This was supposed to be a happy occasion. I was home and I was ready to get my life together and get my family back. So I asked her, "What's your problem? Why are you

so angry?" Camile looked at

me with a face of fury. Then

she cut her eyes to the right at

Shakira, who was peeping

around the corner, and said,

"Kira, go to your room and

close the door." With a

concerned voice I said,

"Baby I don't under..."

Camile interrupted me and said, "Exactly! That's the problem! You don't understand! You never understood! You don't understand because you haven't been here to understand! Do you even realize how long two years is!?! 720 days! Countless hours and minutes! Do you realize how hard it is having to try to stay strong not only for the kids, but for myself?!? Maybe I should go to jail and leave you with two kids to take care of and see if you leave me or not!"

I figured the best thing to do was to let her talk,

but I couldn't even do that

right. "Say something!" She

told me. "I don't know what

to say other than I'm sorry

baby. I promise to do better. I

promise. I know it's going to

be a process and I know you

have already done more than

enough for me, but I promise

if you continue to pray for me

and work with me, we can

work through this. I am going

to do whatever it takes to get

my family back. I don't care

how long it takes and I don't

care what I have to do. I'm

ready, willing and able.

Please baby, work through

this with me." With a face of

willingness and watery eyes

after a sigh she said, "You

can start by washing the

dishes." Then she began to

cry as I wrapped my arms

around her.

"Get off of me!" She

said as she pushed me in the

chest. "It's not that easy! You

are going to have to prove

yourself. You will go to

church! You will get a job!

You will not put your hands

on me! Do you understand

me!?! Most of all, you will

respect me and the kids and

stay off of those drugs and

alcohol!" I felt like a kid that

had gotten in trouble the way

she was yelling at me. "Okay

baby. I understand. Just give

me a chance. I will make this work." Camile looked at me with a death stare. She dried her tears and said, "You have ONE chance."

All I could say was, "Okay." I went and sat out on the porch for a while and thought about what I was going to do the next day. I had a lot to do, and with the

way Camile was going on

and on I didn't have long to

get it all done. I had to get a

job, start going to church and

prove I had changed. None of

them were easy tasks, but I

figured I would work on

showing I had changed first

since I was home. I went in

and found Camile in the

kitchen and asked her, "Baby,

can we have Bible study after

dinner?" She looked at me

surprised at first, then said,

"Um, sure. Don't think that

that's all it's going to take for

you to fix this though."

"Sweetheart I know we have

a long way to go. I just

figured why wait?" Camile

laughed; something I missed

more than anything. "Alright,

Tristen will be here soon so

we can all have dinner then

Bible study."

CHAPTER FIFTEEN: FOR YOURSELF

Within two weeks I landed a job at local restaurant as a waiter. That was definitely something that would further my patience and humble me all the more. After a few days of

father-son time and hours of
silence, Tristen began to talk
to me. I teared up at his first
words to me again. He said,
"Dad, how do I do this math
problem?" I looked at it with
haste and determination. I
became super dad. I knew I
couldn't let him down. This
was his first time putting trust

in me in 2 years. However, it
was something I had never
seen before. I panicked and
became discouraged
internally. Nevertheless, I
tried. I wanted my son back.
So after about 30 seconds of
looking at the problem I said,
"Shoot son, let's google that
thing!" He laughed

uncontrollably and we began

to wrestle and play like a real

father and son would do.

Shakira heard the fun

and did not want to be left

out. She came out of nowhere

and dived straight on top of

us. I couldn't believe it. I was

having fun. To top it all off, I

was having fun with my kids.

Smiling like a schoolgirl who had just been kissed by her crush I looked toward the door of Tristen's room to find Camile standing in the doorway. She shook her head and walked away.

I had already gone to the altar at the church, as I know it is customary to come to Christ if you have

confessed you believe. I

wanted to do everything right

with decency and order

before God and most of all

for my family. Camile and

my kids were right by my

side as I went to the altar and

confessed. The pastor was so

excited about me coming that

they decided to baptize me

that day. I was so happy. So,

since things were going so

well, I did not understand

why Camile was still acting

so strange. I figured her

mother had something to do

with it. So after our playtime

and homework, I sent the

kids into the living room to

watch television while I talked to Camile in the bedroom. Needless to say it didn't go to well.

"Baby, you don't seem happy. What's wrong?" I asked. "You just don't get it do you?" she said. "Get what!?!" I said with anger and confusion. At this point I was finally fed up and my

temper got the best of me. "I

have done everything you

and your mom has asked of

me! I am not on drugs, I

don't drink, I have a job and I

am going to church! What

more do you want from

me!?! I have done everything

to get my family back and

now you mean to tell me you

still want more!?! Everybody

is okay with me but you!

What do you have against

me!?! I know I was gone for

two years, so are you going

to put me through two years

of hell for it!?!" "My mother

has nothing to do with this!"

Camile exclaimed. "So do

you really think coming

home and making a major

turn-around is all it's going to

take to win me over!?! It's

going to take time Shakir!

You know, like the time you

spent in jail away from us!?!

You have no idea what I am

trying to get you to see!" I hit

the wall in fury, "Then

Camile darnitt tell me! Tell

me what I am not

understanding! Tell me what

I am missing! I did all of this

for y'all! I did all of this to

get my family back; I did all

of this to finally be what a

man is supposed to be to you

and my children! I love

y'all!" Camile interrupted,

"That's the point! When you went to the altar, you didn't go for yourself! You went because you knew it was right and that's what you were taught, not because you wanted to! I question your judgement and your heart because of this! How can I be with a man that is easily influenced!?! I don't need you to have God for us! I need you to have God for yourself. That is the only way you're going to able to lead this family!"

A mode of silence came over the room. I felt my heartbeat just like I did when my case commenced back in jail when I was up for parole.

Only this time, I didn't cry. I

didn't smile. I felt void and

lost. I felt empty and

confused. All of this time, I

simply wanted my family

back and God was the way to

do it. Now, my wife won't

accept me because I don't

know him for myself. I only

knew what I was taught. I felt

my mental relapse to past

events that brought my

happiness. I marveled to do

and participate in those

things. I had a taste for a

beer. I reminisced over

shooting up again. As I

looked Camile in the eyes, I

couldn't bear what I saw. I

simply turned around and

walked out of the bedroom.

I didn't know exactly

what I was doing, but I knew

I couldn't be there much

longer without exploding

uncontrollably. So, I packed

my bag and I went to stay at a

hotel not too far from the

house. Upon leaving, I

hugged the kids and told

them the new job required me

to go away for a little while

but I would visit every day. I

felt devastated at the first step

out of the door. It was like

stepping into war. Before I

made that second step

however, Camile said, "I love

you" I couldn't muster up

words, so I gave her a head

nod and closed the door

behind me. My anger built

because she didn't stop me or

even beg for me to stay. It

was as if she didn't care, so

how could she say she loved

me and let me leave so

freely? I would only

understand later.

CHAPTER SIXTEEN:

HOTEL HELL

I called Camile as

soon as I got settled into my

room. She didn't answer as

expected. I laid my bag down

on the bed and went to the

bathroom. It was roach

infested and dirty. I couldn't

complain though. The room

was only 25 dollars a night.

After using the bathroom, I

just sat on the bed and

thought for a while. Then I

proceeded to turn on the

television. I only had one

channel to look at. It was

public television. I tried to

look at the situation on the

bright side. At least if I couldn't sleep I could watch that and fall asleep since it was so boring.

I walked out to the balcony and saw cigarette buds everywhere. I looked down below me in the parking lot to find a man and woman arguing about money.

The man pulled the woman in

the room where I later heard

screams as I reminisced on

the decision I had made to go

to that hotel. Images of

Tristen and Shakira ran

through my mind as tears fell.

I had lost all hope. I figured

this was it for me and this is

where I would end up for the

rest of my life. I would be busting tables and living in a roach-infested rat hole until God called me home. I was thinking this is what I get for all of my sin.

I went back into the room and decided I might as well try to have a little Bible study. Soon, there was a knock at my door. I peeked

and there was a woman I had

never seen before at the door.

So I opened it and said, "Can

I help you ma'am?" She said,

"I'll do you right if you do

me right." "Excuse me?" I

said, knowing now that the

woman is high. "C'mon

Trevor, stop playing and drop

your drawers. Don't even
close the door. You know the
drill. Pay to play!" Mind you,
this woman was indeed not a
bad sight to see, but I am a
married man. "No ma'am," I
said. "You have the wrong
guy." "Oh, I'm sorry." She
says. "You're cute though.
Do you smoke?" "No ma'am.

I'm sorry." I said. "Do you drink? Do you sell?" She asked. I said, "Goodnight ma'am" as I closed the door.

As I sat back on the bed once more ready to open my Bible, I saw three missed calls from Camile. I tried calling back but to no avail. She texted back saying,

"That's fine. I knew you were with someone else. Enjoy yourself. Your family will be waiting for you when you are ready." I was enraged, so I threw the phone on the floor and screamed to the top of my lungs. The devil had used a hooker to keep me from answering my wife and now she thinks I am with someone

else. I felt like I was being

taken to Hell all over again.

This was worse than jail. I

asked myself, "Where is

Tyrone when you need him?"

I fell to my knees and

I didn't know what to say. I

stayed there a while in

silence just

breathing…thinking…reflecti

ng…crying…. My muscles

tightened and all I could do

was get up scream again and

throw things. I was angry.

Then it turned to sadness.

Then it turned to depression.

Then I fell to my knees a

second time. I still didn't

know what to say to God

through the tears and

sobbing. I couldn't get out

words because my heart was

heavy, like a piece of lead

crushing my ribs.

I grabbed the covers

at the foot of the bed where I

was kneeling. I gripped them

until my hands cramped.

Tears fell like Niagara Falls

and flowed like the Nile

River. I shook my head back

and forth because I could not

feel anything but pain from

my past and all of the things I

had done and was sorry for.

All I wanted was my family

back, but they did not want

me. The only thing I could

muster up was, "Lord, please

come see about me," through

my emotions. Then I fell

asleep on the floor, which

was probably not the best

place to be in such a nasty

environment.

CHAPTER SEVENTEEN:

DEPRESSION

I went to work the next morning tired and groggy. I tossed and turned all night long, still reluctant to get off of the floor from some odd reason. I just couldn't get my mind and spirit to relax, not to mention

roaches crawling all over me

all night to top it off. I felt the

bags swollen under my eyes

as the wind hit my face that

morning walking to work. As

soon as I crossed the street to

get to my job, I saw my

mother-in-law ride past me.

She turned around and pulled

up next to me. "Well look

what the devil coughed up."

She said. "Look, don't start."

I told her with a sigh. "What

do you want?" "I didn't want

anything. I just am so happy

you decided to leave my

daughter. You know she is

much better off without you.

She is already dating again.

Soon, y'all will be signing

divorce papers."

My fist tightened

naturally, almost like an

instinct. I breathed slowly

and told her, "Have a good

day mom." She said, "My

name is Eunice! There, I

finally told you." She was

very subconscious about her

name that not too many

people knew her name.

"Eunice…" I said. She said,

"Yes, and don't go around

telling people my name!"

"That was my mother's

name…" I told her. "I think

it's beautiful." She paused

and squinted her eyes at me.

"Just stay away from my

daughter." She said as she

drove off at a fast speed.

Work was killer that

particular day. My patience

was tried heavily that whole

day. From my manager to

customers, it seemed like

everyone was trying to get on

my nerves. One customer

told me I was rude. Another

customer and her family told

me I was not courteous

enough and gave me a small

tip. That morning just threw

my whole day off. I went to

pray in the bathroom stall and

the manager interrupted my

prayer and told me to come

out and keep working. That is

when my anger set in and I

began to lose control.

I proceeded to a table in my area and tried being nice again. The man was by himself and he looked like he was pretty professional. He said to me, "So you're my waiter? I guess you'll do. Get me some water will you?" I couldn't take it anymore.

"Who do you think you're

talking to!?! I said in a loud

voice. My manager

immediately came over, sent

me home for my response,

and served the man himself.

The walk home felt

like I had just been dumped

by my first love. Fortunately,

I was not fired. I was just sent

home and written up. When I

got to the room, I fell face

first on the bed and cried. I

threw my Bible and started to

rip the covers off of my bed. I

went into the bathroom and

looked myself in the dirty

mirror through my tears. I

took my clothes off and just

stood in the shower for a

while in a daze. It was only

cold water, but I was so out

of it that it didn't even matter.

I didn't know what to do or

where to turn. At this point, I

had given up completely. My

wife had moved on. My kids

were probably enjoying a

new stepdad. I figured I

might as well turn to what I

liquor store down the street

from the hotel after returning

the necklace and I also

bought some weed. I didn't

feel like shooting up

anymore. My mind was blank

as I ingested the Jack Daniels

and smoked. It felt so good to

my flesh, but I could not

shake my depressed mood

knew to turn to in times like

this.

I had just gotten paid

a couple of days before. I

bought Camile a diamond

necklace with the money, but

we weren't even on speaking

terms. I decided to take it

back and have some fun with

the money. I went to the

and my low feeling state. The

more I drank and smoked, the

more my mood set in. I

eventually just went to sleep.

Being off the next day helped

tremendously because I was

hungover and was not feeling

well. Camile called that

morning, but I was so sick I

couldn't even reach the

phone. Plus, I had the

mindset of, "Why call me

when you have a new man?"

I was in a bad way…in a low

valley…a dark tunnel not

knowing if I am going

backwards or forward.

CHAPTER EIGHTEEN:

CARNAL CHAOS

After lying in bed for

a while fighting dehydration

and hangover headaches, not

to mention an upset stomach,

I decided to try to call

Camile. The phone went

straight to voicemail. I threw

the phone on the floor and

pulled the cover over my

head. Then, it rang. I

immediately sprang up and

retrieved it from the floor,

only to discover it was the

job calling me. I didn't

answer. I knew they were

calling me to come in. I was

too messed up to go in. I

knew I needed to eat

something, but I didn't have

anything to eat. The closest

eatery was a block away. I

was not sure if I would make

it on my own.

I didn't know what

else to do so I did the only

thing I could do. I started to

pray. "God please help me. If

you get me through this, I promise I will never drink or smoke again." Five minutes later, Camile called me. I rolled over and tried to answer like nothing was wrong in a normal voice. "Hey baby." I said. "Hey." She said. "You sound sick. What's wrong?" I didn't want to lie because I was trying to

do the right thing. "Camile, I

am sick because I drank and

smoked last night. I didn't

know what else to do. I am so

sorry. I just want my family

back. I just want things to be

like they were. Can we get

back to being a family? I

already made God a promise

I will never do this again"

There was silence on
the phone for a while, but I
could tell Camile was crying
on the other end. She sniffed
and said, "Find God Shakir.
Then you will find us." Then
she hung up. I threw the
phone to the wall, but I was
too sick to throw a fit. So, I

just laid there in anger and

despair, longing for days of

old and hoping for a brighter

future with my family still.

After a few hours, I grabbed

my Bible and pulled it close

to my torso. I reminisced

over verses I knew and

finally was able to sleep

comfortably in a sense.

When I woke up, I

was dizzy and I still was not

feeling all the way up to par.

So, I went to the gas station

down the street and bought

some Gatorade, water and

some snacks with the little

money I had. After getting

back to the room and

hydrating, I began to read

random passages in my

Bible. I was trying to figure

out how to get to know God

for myself. Then, it hit me.

Why don't I just go see

Tyrone? He will know what

to do! It was Thursday and

visiting hours were not over

yet. So, I decided to take a

cab down to the jail.

When I got there, I

signed in and waited to meet

with him. The warden came

out and looked at me strange.

I asked him, "Is there a

problem sir?" He looked at

me with sad eyes and said,

"You won't be able to see

Tyrone." I said, "Okay, what

day can I come back and see

him? I have something

important to ask him." The

warden sighed and said, "You

will never be able to see

Tyrone." "Why?" I asked.

The warden relayed to me,

"Tyrone was stabbed to death

a few weeks ago. I'm so

sorry." My mind went

completely blank. All that

was positive was stripped

away from me in an instant

with this news. I wasn't even

saddened. I just turned and

walked away.

I was truly lost now. I

had no guidance and no one

to keep me on the right path.

I had nowhere to turn and

nowhere to go. I was at a

standstill. I cried and ended up walking back to the hotel to try to find some solace along the way. I was so tired that I just collapsed on the floor again when I got there. I mustered up a small prayer as I closed my eyes, "Lord, I have nowhere else to turn. If you can hear me, I need you.

I need to know you for

myself. Teach me how to do

this. In Jesus' name…." Then

I fell asleep.

CHAPTER

NINETEEN: GOD'S PLAN

I woke up and reality

hit me. Tyrone was dead. My

family was only two blocks

away but still so far from me.

I was walking on eggshells

with my job and I had just

relapsed into old habits the

day before. I was so tired of

my situation that I literally

checked out of the hotel and

walked around the city

aimlessly trying to find

answers.

Negativity filled the

air around me as the day went

by. I didn't have much

money to go on, but I know I

didn't want to go back to that

hotel. So many thoughts went

through my head with each

step I took. "Why don't you

just kill yourself? Why are

you even trying? Do you

really think God is going to

show you a way out of this?"

For while I believed this, and

I really thought I was

walking aimlessly, until I

ended up at the doorstep of

the last house I ever thought I

would go to… my

mother-in-law's.

Nightfall had come, and as I knocked on the door, I did not know what to expect. Honestly, I didn't know why I was knocking. I had no intentions on speaking to her or even seeing her. I can only say God led me to her house. Still, I did not know what would go on or what we would have a conversation about.

"Who is it?!" she yelled as she came to the door. She must have peeked into her peephole because she asked, "And just what do you want!?!" The only words I could muster up were, "Can I come in please? I need to talk to you." "What do you want to talk about?!" She asked. Pleading even more I asked again, "Please may I come in?"

A silence filled the air for about 30 seconds, then the door opened slowly. "Come on in." she said. "What are you doing out so late?" Why

are you here?" I had to be

speaking from my heart

because I did not know what

I wanted to talk about but I

knew I needed to get things

off my chest. So, as we sat in

the living room, I told her,

"Listen, I know we haven't

been on the best of terms

ever, but I just wanted to let you know I love you despite our differences. No, Camile does not know I am here, nor did she ask me to come. I don't even know what led me here, but I am here. I just want my family back mama. I just want to do what God wants me to do. I want to live for him and know him

for myself. I guess that is

why he led me here."

She lowered her head

in silence and began to

sniffle. I did not know why

but I could tell she was

crying. A sense of relief

came over me and she lifted

her head again with tears in

her eyes and wiping them

slowly because of her natural

long nails.

"What's wrong

mama? Did I say something

wrong?" She stood up with

her arms out and told me,

"Come here son. I love you

too." After a brief hug we sat

next to one another now. She

finally confided in me as if

we were schoolgirls having a

sleepover. I couldn't

complain however, because

this was the beginning of a

tight bond with the mother I

needed in a mother-in-law.

"When Camile's

father left us, she was all I

had. We were a team. We

did everything together, but I

knew one day a man would

come and take my baby away

from me. I didn't want her

going through the same thing

I went through with her

father. So I automatically had

a hate for you regardless of

how you were. You see,

Camile' father would stay out

all night, be gone all day and

still want to say he loves me

after arguing and even

abusing me sometimes. You

know that man you met in

jail?"

My heart dropped. I

gulped internally and said,

"Yea, you mean Tyrone?

What about him?" She gave

me the stare as if I already

knew what she was going to

say. Then I put two and two

together. She said, "Needless

to say, Camile's father is dead

now, but I am so glad he

turned his life around before

God called him home.

Camile was too young to

remember him, so I never

wanted to tell her about his

situation. One day I just

might. Knowing God put you

two in the same cell angered

me even more and I actually

prayed you wouldn't get out

at first. Then when I saw

your face in that first hearing,

I could tell there was a

change in you. That is when

God started to work on me."

Tears began to roll

down my face uncontrollably.

The very man who showed

me the way to Christ went

down the same path as me

and I had no idea. God truly

works in mysterious ways.

"Don't cry son. It's your

time. Show my daughter

what a real man is. Treat her

right and get to know God for

yourself. He didn't bring you

this far just to give up now.

He led you here. He will lead

you the rest of the way.

I smiled and stood

and said, "Thank you mama,

for everything." As I

grabbed my bag she said,

"Now just where do you

think you're going?" A bit

confused and giddy, I

laughed and before I could

make words, she said, "I

cooked and there is no one

here to eat and I have a guest

room that needs to be broken

in. So you sit yourself down

and get comfortable while I

fix you a plate." Needless to

say I was being held captive

at my mother-in-law's house.

I had no complaints however.

It 100 times better than the

streets or a roach-infested

hotel.

CHAPTER

TWENTY: TIME TO GO

My supervisor noticed

I was doing much better and

asked me if I wanted to make

some extra hours in the

coming weeks. Of course I

told him yes and he also

complimented my

appearance. He said I looked much less stressed and a lot more positive. That was motivation to keep me going.

When I got off, mom rode me around for a while and we talked. "What do you want to do in life? she asked. "I don't know now mom," I said. " I didn't know much more than working at the

plant all those years before,”

Before I could continue she

interrupted and said, “So

what do you like to do?” I

had to ponder and I could

think of nothing. “I don’t

know mom. As a kid, I used

to love writing.” “What made

you stop?” she asked. “One

of my teachers asked me

what I wanted to do when I

grew up. I told her I wanted

to write. She told me there

was not much money in it, so

I let that dream go."

Mom shook her head,

sighed and said, "Baby

follow your heart and chase

your dreams. Don't let

anyone stop you from achieving and attaining. I have faith in you." Those words sent a shock through my body and I immediately wanted to write. I started something that night, but I did not want to be late for church the next day, so I cut it short.

Church had already

begun by the time I got there.

Mom went to a different

church so she dropped me

off. "Remember, go when

God tells you to. Don't go

any sooner and don't go any

later." I kept that on the

forefront of my mind as I

entered doors to the

sanctuary.

Strangely, I sat in the back like most who don't wish to be seen. Pastor spoke with such power and eloquence that I was forced to listen. The word was hitting me all over and I could not sit still. I sweated, I cried and I even trembled.

When the doors of the church

were open, I felt an inward

pull. I stood out in the aisle

and paused before I made a

step. My first step felt like

cement was in my shoes.

With my second step heads

started to turn because people

noticed that I was coming

down the aisle. At first it felt

like a walk of shame until I

heard applause and praise.

When I got to the

front were the Pastor was

standing, he asked me what I

was coming for. Then he

handed me the microphone. I

didn't know exactly what to

say, so just like at mom's

house, I spoke from the heart.

Before I began to speak, her

words rang in my ears, "He

led you here. He will lead

you the rest of the way."

"Good morning church." I

said. " I am not sure what I

am about to say but I do

know that I want to know

God for myself and I have

been led here by him. After

drugs, jail and losing my

family and all solace and in

anyone or anything else, God

is truly all I have right now. I

need him and I pray that you

all pray for me and with me

as I try to get it together. I do

wish to be baptized and I do

wish to grow in the Lord."

As I finished my

statement, I turned around after Pastor prayed over me and Camile was standing there in tears along with my children. She put her arms around me and hugged me like she did at the end of our first date. She gazed into my eyes and I knew at that moment I had my family back. She smiled, turned her

head slightly to the right and

said, "Let's go home." Those

words never sounded so

good.

CHAPTER TWENTY-ONE: SWEETER AND SWEETER

So there you have it. That's my story. I was a man who didn't know God, didn't care about God and now God is my all in all. I have learned that you have to be open and receptive in order to achieve

and attain anything. Most

importantly you have to have

love in order for anything in

your life to flourish. I had so

many blessings right in my

face for years and never even

knew it. I am regretful for the

time I wasted but I am so

grateful for the time I have

and the time I was given to

get it right.

I also know now that I

have to know God for myself.

I can't make it to heaven off

of my family's faith.

Needless to say I am teaching

my children the same and I

pray they teach their children

as well. My wife and I are

finally one, equally yoked

and walking this Christian

journey together side by side.

I truly thank her for being all

that she has been and is being

to me.

     I also thank God for

my mother-in-law for the

good and bad she brought

into my life. It allowed to

grow into the man I am
today. She also told me to
chase my dreams, which is
why you are reading this
story. Anyway, I hear my
wife calling my name. It
must be time for dinner.
Thanks for listening. Be
blessed.